Does God Care What We
wear?

cary schmidt

Striving Together Publications
4020 E. Lancaster Blvd.
Lancaster, CA 93535
800.201.7748

Cover design by Andrew Jones
Layout by Craig Parker
Special thanks to our editorial team and proofreaders.

ISBN 978-1-59894-087-9

Printed in the United States of America

People often wonder and ask about dress standards for Christians. Does God really care about our clothing? Should we have a dress standard? If so, what should it be? How do we determine it? Why should we have one? The questions and the accompanying opinions sometimes seem endless, and can actually distract from the central point of the Christian life and ministry. This is a confusing issue among Christians in the twenty-first century and many are looking for balanced, biblical answers.

As culture continually slips into sloppier and sleazier, many churches and families have all but given up this battle. Many are opting for the "God loves us no matter how we dress" approach to Christianity. And of course He does! No one argues that point. But God loves me regardless of how I *live* too! That argument just isn't valid when considering "what to wear." God's love or acceptance isn't the issue—pleasing Him and representing Him well are the issues.

In the next several pages, we will explore the subject of dress from a biblical perspective. If you are a new Christian, perhaps these thoughts will encourage you to more carefully and deliberately represent your Saviour in your dress choices. If you are a parent, perhaps this study will encourage you to implement biblical principles for your children and your own home. If you are a spiritual leader or pastor, perhaps you will consider reasonably defining your ministry's dress guidelines, and compassionately lead others to honor the Lord. In any case, I hope we all decide to "raise the bar" for some very good biblical reasons. I believe the Bible is very clear—*yes*—God does care what we wear.

In Matthew 11:7–9 Jesus is speaking about John the Baptist—"... *What went ye out into the wilderness to see? A reed shaken with the wind? But what went ye out for to see? A man clothed in soft raiment? behold, they that wear soft clothing are in kings' houses. But what went ye out for to see? A prophet? yea, I say unto you, and more than a prophet."*

While clothing is not the central context of this passage, Jesus draws a clear distinction between the clothing of a godly man and the clothing worn in a pagan environment—kings' houses. The terms *soft raiment* and *soft clothing* in this passage refers to "clothing of uncertain affinity" or "effeminate clothing"—frankly referencing the common homosexual practices that took place in "kings' houses." The Bible draws the same type of contrast in Proverbs 7:10 where it says, "…*the attire of an harlot.*" The point is—different types of people dress differently, and clothing always identifies us with a lifestyle. To put one application of these verses in plain English, godly men should not dress the same as effeminate men, and godly ladies should not dress like harlots.

Would you consider with me your dress choices? Would you evaluate what you allow your family to wear in a variety of contexts, and would you let those decisions be subject to God's will? If so, then I pray that the following points will challenge your thinking and provoke serious consideration of this matter. I recently gave our church families and youth workers eleven reasons why we should develop a personal as well as a ministry dress standard—the same reasons I have a dress standard for my family.

1.   To please the Lord Jesus Christ and honor Him above all.

So many of our dress decisions are entirely based on pleasing self and pleasing others. When you get dressed, for whom are you dressing? First Corinthians 10:31 teaches, *"Whether therefore ye eat, or drink, or whatsoever ye do, do all to the glory of God."* Jesus also said, *"…I do always those things that please him"* (John 8:29). Every decision you make, including what you put on in the morning, should be based first and foremost upon this criteria: What pleases my God?

2.   To submit to the biblical principle of modesty.

This is more of an issue with ladies because men are "sight oriented." If you have a home with only girls, you may not naturally understand this issue because you don't think like a man. What some ladies think is "cute" is very often provocative in the eyes of a man. Dads must be the authority in this area and moms should work to educate themselves on what their daughters look like through the eyes of young men. First Timothy 2:9 teaches, *"In like manner also, that women adorn themselves in modest apparel…."* This is not to say we shouldn't try to look nice or fashionable, but simply that modesty should be a higher priority and a constant consideration.

3. To submit to the biblical principle of appropriateness and to identify with godliness.

Philippians 4:5 teaches, *"Let your moderation be known unto all men. The Lord is at hand."* The definition of *moderation* is *appropriateness.* While young men might not have to grapple so much with the modesty issue, they certainly should be taught what is *appropriate* dress for various environments.

It seems our young people are being taught that wearing their "ball-game" clothing to church is appropriate. It simply isn't. And in many cases those in leadership seem to lead the charge toward sloppiness in dress. When it comes to our appearance, we should dress with a higher respect and esteem for *spiritual environments* than we do for mowing the lawn or attending a ball game. Respect is the reason we dress better for weddings and funerals—we respect the *people* and the *environment* involved. We respect what is happening in these settings so we dress better for them. Why should the Lord and His work receive less respect than the dead?

Why should spiritual environments be thought of as less significant or respectable than secular environments? When we allow this sort of duplicity, the subtle message to the next generation is that we really don't value the things that God values the same way He does.

4. To promote an environment of purity and spiritual growth.

Sadly, young people today are more sexually educated, sexually tempted, and sexually active than they have *ever* been in American history! In our homes and churches, we should be committed to maintaining a pure and godly atmosphere—meaning dress should be modest and appropriate. It should honor the Lord and reflect a high view of Him. The way we dress absolutely contributes to the environment of a group or family setting, and these environments should be godly and Christ-honoring.

Additionally, many people draw much of their identity from their clothing! Because they are highly self-conscious and image conscious, they try to create an identity with specific clothing lines and designer names. Read this statement carefully: A group dynamic (as a youth group) where every individual is consumed with social status and fashion trends doesn't lend itself to individual spiritual growth.

Every time our youth group meets, we are pursuing spiritual transformation in young lives. This is not a light endeavor. It is a very serious undertaking. And our dress should contribute to the process, not detract or interfere with it. Romans 13:14, *"But put ye on the Lord Jesus Christ, and make not provision for the flesh, to fulfil the lusts thereof."* Romans 14:19, *"Let us therefore follow after the things which make for peace, and things wherewith one may edify another."*

Relate this scenario to the *environment* principle: What if your child needed open heart surgery and the surgeon showed up for surgery smelling like sunscreen, wearing flip flops, cut-off shorts, a tank top, a ball cap, sunglasses? You would deem him inappropriate and unfit for surgery!

When my daughter was born she was eight weeks early, and for two weeks she had to be kept in the NICU ward of the hospital. Strangely, every time I wanted to hold her or see her, I had to scrub my hands and arms and cover myself in an odd-looking blue outfit. Why? Because the NICU is a delicate health environment where little lives are at stake. The value of those lives places a premium on the cleanliness of the environment.

So, how valuable are the young hearts we are raising in today's godless culture? How safe and pure is the environment you create in your home or church? Is your home, church, and youth group a place where spiritual growth is highly valued? Or is it a place where sensuality reigns in the name of "grace"? I know that's a strong implication, but I fear that we have devalued our spiritual environments to the point that, though church might be fun—dressing trendy, dancing, and celebrating—we have killed the chance for real life transformation. Environment matters, and clothing definitely contributes to an environment.

5. *To honor the convictions or preferences of others.*

If you have been on this planet very long, you're probably figuring out that it is comprised of many different cultures. Several years ago, I had the privilege of participating in a Spiritual Leadership Conference hosted in Seoul, South Korea. For a week we enjoyed sweet fellowship, music, teaching, and preaching with faithful Korean Christians. It was amazing!

Throughout the week, I was subjected to customs and cultural preferences that were Korean—things we just don't do in America. For instance, every time we visited a home, we were asked to take off our shoes. And every time we ate dinner in a home, we sat on the floor to do so.

Honestly, these customs were not my preferences. And frankly, I had every right to refuse and resist. Yet, it was love and respect for my fellow Christians that caused me to "prefer others." I didn't argue or debate. I didn't gossip and get a bad attitude. I didn't even consider the Korean Christians to be legalists. I simply accepted their preferences and cultural practice. And in respect and decency, I honored their wishes.

What could possibly be wrong with simply preferring another person—especially one in spiritual authority like a parent, a pastor, or a teacher? The Bible is clear on this principle in two ways. First, we are commanded to honor those who have the rule over us. Hebrews 13:17, *"Obey them that have the rule over you, and submit yourselves: for they watch for your souls...."* Second, we are commanded to prefer one another in love. Romans 12:10, *"Be kindly affectioned one to another with brotherly love; in honour preferring one another."*

This principle is not about founding your personal convictions upon the whims of another person. Quite the contrary, it's about simply showing basic human decency for the preferences of a person you love and respect. (And honestly, if reading these words tweaks your spirit a little bit, that's probably the sign of a wrong heart toward another Christian.) Respecting another's preference is not mindless submission—it is mature, loving decency.

Not long ago, I was visiting a golf course clubhouse in jeans and a t-shirt. As I approached the front door, a sign stated: "Attention Guests— Appropriate dress is casual pants and collared shirt. No shorts or T-shirts are permitted." While I could have rebelled at the preference of the golf-course management, I didn't. I simply went home to change, and returned to the golf course dressed appropriately. That's just basic human decency.

For young people, the question of dress is as simple as, What do my parents, pastors, and teachers want me to wear? The attitude that says "I'll wear what I want no matter what anybody says" is not only rebellious, it is just purely selfish and childish. Any two year old can display this sort of defiance on cue. If I know that an authority figure prefers that I dress a certain way, I'm right to honor and to prefer my authority just to show love and respect.

Question: Why will we honor employers, restaurants, golf courses, and bowling alleys (Yes, I'll explain that one later), but we won't honor the Lord or environments that represent Him? When I was sixteen working at McDonald's, they made me wear a blue hat! I didn't like it. I didn't want to wear it. I thought it was stupid. But I wore it—with a good attitude. Why? Because they paid me.

6. *To give an account to the Lord with joy.*

This point is really big for those in leadership—parents, pastors, etc. We really do have to stand before God to answer for the environment we allow as leaders. We will answer to God for what we allow and teach—even inadvertently. May God give us the courage to make our dress choices, not based on the shifting trends of culture, but on the principle of accountability to God. Second Corinthians 5:10, *"For we must all appear before the judgment seat of Christ; that every one may receive the things done in his body, according to that he hath done, whether it be good or bad."*

7. *To promote spiritual maturity.*

Maturity isn't measured by age, but by the acceptance of responsibility. Everybody has influence, and the young people we influence are quickly becoming adults. No responsible adult gets to dress the way he wants all the time. Mature adults accept boundaries in a multitude of environments—because they take responsibility seriously.

When leaders promote a "wear whatever I want" mentality, they foster a self-centered mindset—a "the world revolves around me" way of thinking. Maturity and responsibility see dress and appearance as one aspect of influence, and accept the responsibility of being a godly influence upon others.

It is possible to help this generation of young people understand what it means to be mature examples. In fact, God commands in 1 Timothy 4:12, *"Let no man despise thy youth; but be thou an example of the believers, in word, in conversation, in charity, in spirit, in faith, in purity."*

8. *To exemplify a distinct lifestyle that is not conformed to the world.*

Simply put, the attitude that says, "I can wear what I want when I want, and nobody can tell me different" is not a spiritual life—it's a carnal life. This life is *conformed,* not *transformed.* Ephesians 5:8, *"For ye were sometimes darkness, but now are ye light in the Lord: walk as children of light."* Romans 12:2, *"And be not conformed to this world: but be ye transformed by the renewing of your mind, that ye may prove what is that good, and acceptable, and perfect, will of God."*

I still believe that God intends for us to walk "out of step" with the world. This simply isn't the practice for modern Christendom. Most Christians are trying the best way they can to blend in with the world's styles. Why do we care what the world thinks more than what the Lord desires? God instructs us in Galatians that, even as we are in Christ, we are also to put on Christ. Most Christians are more than happy to be *in* Christ, but far fewer really desire to *put on* Christ.

9. *To protect the thoughts and innocence of others.*

No parents would want young men lusting after their daughter. No parents would want their son tempted by the dress of others. Unfortunately, during their teen years, our sons will most likely see, by accident, more inappropriate clothing than their grandfathers could have looked for in a lifetime.

For this reason, a Christian environment (such as a church service or a home fellowship with friends) should be a "spiritually-safe" environment. When we teach modesty to young women, we are teaching them to value themselves as God does and to save themselves for marriage, and we are protecting the hearts and minds of young men— helping them to guard their thoughts. When we teach appropriateness to young men, we are teaching them responsibility and respect toward the Lord and others.

Second Timothy 2:22 says, *"Flee also youthful lusts: but follow righteousness, faith, charity, peace, with them that call on the Lord out of a pure heart."*

Proverbs 4:23 tells us to, *"Keep thy heart with all diligence; for out of it are the issues of life."*

10.   *To be a clear witness of the Gospel.*

You would have to take several dozen teenagers to public places on a regular basis to understand this example. When appropriately dressed Christian teenagers pile out of a church bus in a McDonalds parking lot, or stand in line together at a theme park—they are noticed. They flat out *shine*!

God commands us to be a peculiar people (Titus 2:14, 1 Peter 2:9). This doesn't mean we are to be strange, but that we are to be set apart to God in contrast to the world around us. Second Corinthians 6:17, *"Wherefore come out from among them, and be ye separate, saith the Lord...."* This principle touches so many areas of our lives. The question is this: in what ways are you different from the world around you? In what ways do you stand in contrast—radiating godliness? In what ways does your light shine?

As Christians, our appearance should be but a small part of what sets us apart from the rest of our culture. We should be His ambassadors, appearing as a representative of God to those around us. We should be epistles *"known and read of all men"* (2 Corinthians 3:2).

Many Christians are willing to advertise sports teams, clothing brands, and secular corporations on what they wear. How much more willing should we be to appear godly—to dress the part of a child of the King.

Not long ago, we had a group of one hundred senior-highers at an In-N-Out Burger (a Southern California favorite restaurant). Our group spent forty-five minutes enjoying food and fellowship. They were dressed sharp, they acted respectfully, and they were kind to others in the restaurant. (For instance, our teens allow other people to take the front of the line whenever our entire group is at a restaurant.) Toward the end of our visit, two adults approached me and asked where these "wonderful students" were from. I happily said, "Lancaster Baptist Church," to which they replied, "Well, this sure gives us hope for the next generation! What a great group of young people!"

I was so thankful for the testimony that the Lord allowed us to have at that moment. Sadly, I've seen youth groups that were in no way different from any other group of teens in secular America. Why can't we remember that man always looks on the outward appearance (1 Samuel 16:7)? Jesus taught us in Matthew 5:16, *"Let your light so shine before men, that they may see your good works, and glorify your Father which is in heaven."*

11. To create a clear distinction of Christian manhood and womanhood.

As we began this booklet, we saw that Jesus drew a contrast in clothing, indicating distinction. Clothing identifies us. It identifies our lifestyles, our attitudes, our personalities, and often our values. Many employers require employees to wear certain uniforms. This policy creates distinction—a clear line between employees and guests. If you don't believe me, just put on a red collared shirt, and walk around Target. It will be only a few moments before someone asks you a question—mistaking you for a Target associate. This is the principle of distinction in action.

What you wear distinguishes you. If you are a woman wearing that which is masculine, you are blurring the distinctiveness of your gender. The same would be true for men wearing effeminate clothing. And while our culture is working hard to blur the lines of distinction between genders, the Bible makes those distinctions very clear. As Christians, may we honor God's design of a masculine and feminine gender, and not obscure the lines between them.

You don't have to look much farther than the picture signs on the doors of public restrooms to know that even culture finds it helpful to distinguish between men and women. As Christians, let's continue to restore and uplift that good, God-given distinction.

Genesis 1:27, *"So God created man in his own image, in the image of God created he him; male and female created he them."*

So there you have them—eleven principles to validate that God does care about what we wear. I pray you will appropriate them and teach them. Everybody knows that dress matters. It's really just a matter of submitting our selfish wills to God and living to please Him first.

These same principles would apply to hairstyles, make-up, manners, and other areas of outward conduct as well. Perhaps as you read these principles you thought, "Well, that's just not ME. I have to be ME." May I gently encourage you to give up that self-centered thought process. I figured out a long time ago that "being myself" was a losing proposition—and a very limiting one. The winning life is really about surrendering your identity fully to Jesus Christ.

Just trust the Lord and His Word. If you are a spiritual leader, lead your group down the right path, communicating clear biblical direction. If you're a Christian, value yourself, your testimony, and your future enough to dress for God's glory. Set aside your own preferences and self-centered thinking. Decide to dress in a way that absolutely pleases the Lord and shows respect for Him in every environment.

In closing, I would like to contextualize everything I've stated earlier with some final thoughts. Encouraging Christians to dress to honor the Lord is not about legalism or arrogance. Some Christians' dress standards will be different from others. We shouldn't look down on someone who doesn't dress exactly to our standard or preference. We should be compassionate and respectful toward them and try to be a godly influence on them.

As you raise the bar in this area, please do so with tenderness and compassion. Teach the truth with love and patience. Decent dress doesn't produce a right heart—it should reflect one. Christ-honoring dress should be the product of a pure heart, not the white-washed exterior of a proud one.

I haven't tried to define your standard in these pages. That's up to you, the Lord, and His Word. If you are a young person, it's up to your authorities. Your standard may not be mine. I'm not accountable for you. My standard doesn't define spirituality; it merely evidences what God has placed on my heart for the environments and people that I influence. You must define your standard by God's leading and be prepared to answer to Him for it.

Not long ago I was with my family strolling through an open shopping area when we happened upon a new bowling alley that served lunch at each lane. We needed lunch and bowling sounded fun; so a few moments later, we were bowling, eating, and making some great memories. It wasn't until we were leaving that I noticed a large sign at the entrance explaining the dress code. I read this sign in disbelief.

The rules were as follows: *No sweatshirts or sports jerseys, no jogging pants or jumpsuits, no MC colors, no hats or headgear, no baggy clothing, all clothing must be neat and clean, no long shorts, no boots, no long or baggy T-shirts, no sleeveless shirts, and no solid color T-shirts.* Wow! All that just for bowling!

Think about that bowling alley. The management there really respects that environment. When it comes to dress, do you care as much about honoring the Lord as they do about bowling?

There is often debate among Christians about standards of living and there is a pervasive thought among Christians today that says, "I will do as I please, because I am under grace." Whether in music, dress, lifestyle, entertainment, or even morals, many have adopted a "have it your way" brand of Christian living under the guise that God cares only about our hearts.

The fault in this thinking is that God gives such clear biblical instruction on our *lifestyle*—commanding us to live in godliness and holiness. This lifestyle is one of *integrity—authenticity*—being the same on the outside as you are on the inside. A godly heart should produce a godly lifestyle—a life that truly *"walks worthy."* Yet, in this day, many Christians disregard their calling that they might *"live unto themselves"* (2 Corinthians 5:15).

Recently, I had the privilege of visiting the Tomb of the Unknown Soldier in Arlington National Cemetery near Washington DC. While our group made its way up the hill toward the tomb, we looked up some information on the guards. As we read, we were amazed at the requirements the Army has placed on all those who would serve in the sacred capacity of guarding the tomb. This position of service is no small responsibility or honor, and with it comes a great degree of personal commitment and sacrifice. These are some of the requirements for tomb guards:

- *Guards are required to memorize sixteen pages of information about Arlington Cemetery.*

- *Guards are required to know the locations and names of three hundred graves.*

- *Guards are required to shave twice daily.*

- *Guards cut their hair every two days—on their day off.*

- *Guards are required to pass a one hundred question test, a uniform test, and a guard change sequence test.*

- *The badge awarded after passing the test can be revoked if guards ever dishonor their oath.*

- *Guards must be between 5'10" and 6'4" in height.*

- *A guard's waste size cannot exceed thirty inches.*

- *Guards must commit two years of their lives to guarding the tomb.*

- *During their service, guards must live in barracks under the tomb.*

- *Guards cannot drink alcohol on or off duty for the rest of their lives.*

- *Guards make a vow not to swear in public for the rest of their lives.*

- *During his first six months, a guard cannot speak to anyone or watch TV.*

- *Off duty time is spent studying the 175 notable people laid to rest in Arlington.*

- *Guards take five to six hours to prepare their uniforms.*

- *A guard's uniform must be completely free of wrinkles, folds, or lint.*

- *A guard's uniform is solid wool and is worn year-round regardless of temperature.*

- *Guards are on duty regardless of weather conditions (including hurricanes).*

- *There is a meticulous twenty-one step ritual with a twenty-one second pause that is carefully repeated.*

- *There is a detailed changing of the guard procedure that is followed precisely.*

- *The procedures are followed whether spectators are viewing or not.*

Isn't it amazing how particular the Army is in the appearance and distinction of a tomb guard? What a stark contrast to the spirit of modern day Christians in the army of the Lord. It should convict us to think that these honorable men would take such an oath and pay such a price to "walk worthy" of their calling—all to guard the tomb of a deceased soldier. Should we not then be willing to "walk worthy of our calling" for a *living Saviour?!*

May God help us to recognize the high calling and responsibility that we have to be His ambassadors on this earth! May we represent Him, not as we please, but as He pleases.

> *"No man that warreth entangleth himself with the affairs of this life; that he may please him who hath chosen him to be a soldier."*
> —2 TIMOTHY 2:4

"That ye would walk worthy of God, who hath called you unto his kingdom and glory."
—1 THESSALONIANS 2:12

"That ye might walk worthy of the Lord unto all pleasing...."—COLOSSIANS 1:10

ABOUT THE AUTHOR

 Cary Schmidt is an associate pastor at Lancaster Baptist Church (Lancaster, California) where he leads the student ministries, music ministry, and media and publications ministry. He and his wife Dana have three children. Together they have devoted their lives to serving families and helping young adults prepare for a lifetime commitment to Jesus Christ. His other books include *Discover Your Destiny, Hook, Line & Sinker, Just Friends,* and *Done.*

The Biblical Sanctity of Life

When does life begin? Nobody wants to answer this question. Our courts cannot decide. Our government cannot decide. Our educational institutions cannot decide. Even our pulpits are growing more and more silent on the value of life in the womb. But God answered this question a long time ago. Have you ever heard His thoughts on the matter? This booklet opens the pages of the Bible and allows God to clearly and powerfully answer the question—when does life begin? (40 pages, booklet)

Exposing the Deception of Humanism

Humanism is the belief that man is his own god, and outside of mankind, we need no higher deity or authority. Proponents of humanism are active in government and education, attempting to remove God from society. This booklet exposes the emptiness behind the message that mankind is his own savior, and it charts a path away from the error and back to the truth of Jesus Christ. Learn the core beliefs of this growing religious movement, and discover how to reject its deception. (48 pages, booklet)

The Blessings and Pitfalls of Social Networking

In this booklet, we examine two angles of social networking—some of the potential blessings and many of the potential pitfalls. We conclude our study by applying several timeless scriptural principles to this emerging technology. (48 pages, booklet)

Visit us online

strivingtogether.com

dailyintheword.org

wcbc.edu

lancasterbaptist.org

paulchappell.com